DISNEP
CLUB PENGUIN
MAD LIBS®

By Roger Price and Leonard Stern

PSS!
PRICE STERN SLOAN

PRICE STERN SLOAN
Published by the Penguin Group
Penguin Group (USA) Inc., 375 Hudson Street, New York, New York 10014, USA
Penguin Group (Canada), 90 Eglinton Avenue East, Suite 700,
Toronto, Ontario M4P 2Y3, Canada
(a division of Pearson Penguin Canada Inc.)
Penguin Books Ltd., 80 Strand, London WC2R 0RL, England
Penguin Group Ireland, 25 St. Stephen's Green, Dublin 2, Ireland
(a division of Penguin Books Ltd.)
Penguin Group (Australia), 250 Camberwell Road, Camberwell, Victoria 3124, Australia
(a division of Pearson Australia Group Pty. Ltd.)
Penguin Books India Pvt. Ltd., 11 Community Centre,
Panchsheel Park, New Delhi—110 017, India
Penguin Group (NZ), 67 Apollo Drive, Rosedale, North Shore 0632, New Zealand
(a division of Pearson New Zealand Ltd.)
Penguin Books (South Africa) (Pty.) Ltd., 24 Sturdee Avenue,
Rosebank, Johannesburg 2196, South Africa

Penguin Books Ltd., Registered Offices:
80 Strand, London WC2R 0RL, England

Published by Price Stern Sloan,
a division of Penguin Young Readers Group,
345 Hudson Street, New York, New York 10014.

ISBN 978-0-8431-3244-1

7 9 10 8

INSTRUCTIONS

MAD LIBS® is a game for people who don't like games!
It can be played by one, two, three, four, or forty.

• RIDICULOUSLY SIMPLE DIRECTIONS

In this tablet you will find stories containing blank spaces where words
are left out. One player, the READER, selects one of these stories. The
READER does not tell anyone what the story is about. Instead, he/she asks
the other players, the WRITERS, to give him/her words. These words are
used to fill in the blank spaces in the story.

• TO PLAY

The READER asks each WRITER in turn to call out a word—an adjective or
a noun or whatever the space calls for—and uses them to fill in the blank
spaces in the story. The result is a MAD LIBS® game.

When the READER then reads the completed MAD LIBS® game to the other
players, they will discover that they have written a story that is fantastic,
screamingly funny, shocking, silly, crazy, or just plain dumb—depending
upon which words each WRITER called out.

• EXAMPLE (*Before* and *After*)

"_____!" he said _____
      EXCLAMATION   ADVERB

as he jumped into his shiny red _____ and
            NOUN

drove off with his _____ friend.
       ADJECTIVE

"_____*Ouch*_____!" he said _____*stupidly*_____
      EXCLAMATION   ADVERB

as he jumped into his shiny red _____*cat*_____ and
            NOUN

drove off with his _____*brave*_____ friend.
       ADJECTIVE

MAD LIBS®

QUICK REVIEW

In case you have forgotten what adjectives, adverbs, nouns, and verbs are, here is a quick review:

An ADJECTIVE describes something or somebody. *Lumpy*, *soft*, *ugly*, *messy*, and *short* are adjectives.

An ADVERB tells how something is done. It modifies a verb and usually ends in "ly." *Modestly*, *stupidly*, *greedily*, and *carefully* are adverbs.

A NOUN is the name of a person, place, or thing. *Sidewalk*, *umbrella*, *bridle*, *bathtub*, and *nose* are nouns.

A VERB is an action word. *Run*, *pitch*, *jump*, and *swim* are verbs. Put the verbs in past tense if the directions say PAST TENSE. *Ran*, *pitched*, *jumped*, and *swam* are verbs in the past tense.

When we ask for A PLACE, we mean any sort of place: a country or city (*Spain*, *Cleveland*) or a room (*bathroom*, *kitchen*).

An EXCLAMATION or SILLY WORD is any sort of funny sound, gasp, grunt, or outcry, like *Wow!*, *Ouch!*, *Whomp!*, *Ick!*, and *Gadzooks!*

When we ask for specific words, like a NUMBER, a COLOR, an ANIMAL, or a PART OF THE BODY, we mean a word that is one of those things, like *seven*, *blue*, *horse*, or *head*.

When we ask for a PLURAL, it means more than one. For example, *cat* pluralized is *cats*.

MAD LIBS® is fun to play with friends, but you can also play it by yourself! To begin with, DO NOT look at the story on the page below. Fill in the blanks on this page with the words called for. Then, using the words you have selected, fill in the blank spaces in the story.

Now you've created your own hilarious MAD LIBS® game!

A TOUR OF CLUB PENGUIN

ADJECTIVE _____

PERSON IN ROOM _____

NOUN _____

ADJECTIVE _____

NOUN _____

PLURAL NOUN _____

TYPE OF LIQUID _____

NOUN _____

NOUN _____

ADJECTIVE _____

ADJECTIVE _____

ADJECTIVE _____

NOUN _____

ADJECTIVE _____

ADJECTIVE _____

MAD LIBS®

A TOUR OF CLUB PENGUIN

Hi, _____ penguins! I'm your tour guide,
         ADJECTIVE

_____, and I am going to show you around
   PERSON IN ROOM

Club Penguin. Right now, we are in the Ski Village, at the base of

the _____ Mountain. Here, you can stop into the Sport
            NOUN

Shop to get some _____ gear, or head to the
                       ADJECTIVE

Ski Lodge to play a game of *Find* _____. Next, let's
                                           NOUN

waddle over to the Town Center, which is always bustling with

_____. You can grab a hot cup of _____
   PLURAL NOUN   TYPE OF LIQUID

at the Coffee Shop, dance the _____ away at the
                                     NOUN

Night Club, or buy a/an _____ at the Gift Shop. The final
                              NOUN

stop on our tour is the Plaza. It's full of _____ things to
                                                ADJECTIVE

do: The Pizza Parlor has _____ pizza, The Stage is famous
                              ADJECTIVE

for its _____ productions, and at the Pet Shop, you can
           ADJECTIVE

adopt a furry _____. Now, go ahead and explore this
                    NOUN

_____ island of endless fun and adventure. There's lots
   ADJECTIVE

more to see! Thanks for coming on my _____ tour!
                                             ADJECTIVE

FROM DISNEY CLUB PENGUIN™ MAD LIBS® • © 2009 Disney. Published by Price Stern Sloan,
a division of Penguin Young Readers Group, 345 Hudson Street, New York, NY 10014.

MAD LIBS® is fun to play with friends, but you can also play it by yourself! To begin with, DO NOT look at the story on the page below. Fill in the blanks on this page with the words called for. Then, using the words you have selected, fill in the blank spaces in the story.

Now you've created your own hilarious MAD LIBS® game!

Q&A WITH ROCKHOPPER

ADJECTIVE _____

ADJECTIVE _____

ADJECTIVE _____

VERB ENDING IN "ING" _____

ADJECTIVE _____

ADJECTIVE _____

PART OF THE BODY _____

A PLACE _____

NOUN _____

NOUN _____

PLURAL NOUN _____

ADJECTIVE _____

NOUN _____

The following is a/an _____ interview with everyone's
ADJECTIVE

favorite pirate penguin, Rockhopper:

Q: Hi, Rockhopper. How are you doing on this _____ day?
ADJECTIVE

A: Ahoy, me hearty! I be feelin' _____. The sun is
ADJECTIVE

_____, and it be a perfect day to sail at sea in me
VERB ENDING IN "ING"

_____ ship, the *Migrator*.
ADJECTIVE

Q: Is that _____ red puffle sitting on your
ADJECTIVE

_____ the one and only Yarr?
PART OF THE BODY

A: Aye, it is! Yarr is me best mate in all of (the) _____.
A PLACE

He be a good lookout on me ship, especially when a/an

_____ is brewing at sea.
NOUN

Q: Are you planning to visit Club _____ anytime soon?
NOUN

A: Well, shiver me _____! I thought ye'd never ask.
PLURAL NOUN

Me supply of cream soda is runnin' low, so I'll be visiting ye

_____ landlubbers soon! Until then, yo-ho, yo-ho, it's
ADJECTIVE

a/an _____'s life for me!
NOUN

MAD LIBS® is fun to play with friends, but you can also play it by yourself! To begin with, DO NOT look at the story on the page below. Fill in the blanks on this page with the words called for. Then, using the words you have selected, fill in the blank spaces in the story.

Now you've created your own hilarious MAD LIBS® game!

ASK AUNT ARCTIC

ADJECTIVE _____

PLURAL NOUN _____

PLURAL NOUN _____

PERSON IN ROOM _____

SAME PERSON IN ROOM _____

ADJECTIVE _____

NOUN _____

NOUN _____

ADJECTIVE _____

ADJECTIVE _____

MAD LIBS®
ASK AUNT ARCTIC

Aunt Arctic's _____ advice column in *The Club*
                    ADJECTIVE

Penguin Times is full of helpful tips. Here is an example:

Dear Aunt Arctic,

I've seen _____ trying to tip the Iceberg. They even
            PLURAL NOUN

have Iceberg-tipping parties! Some drill away at it with jackhammers

and construction _____! Can the Iceberg really be
                   PLURAL NOUN

tipped?

-_____
  PERSON IN ROOM

Dear _____,
       SAME PERSON IN ROOM

I've been asked this _____ question a lot. Actually,
                      ADJECTIVE

I've attended lots of tipping parties. But I've never seen proof

that the Ice-_____ has tipped. But, anything is
              NOUN

possible on Club _____! Perhaps you could start your
                  NOUN

own tipping party. Wouldn't it be _____ to be one of
                                   ADJECTIVE

the first penguins to witness such a/an _____ event?
                                         ADJECTIVE

FROM DISNEY CLUB PENGUIN™ MAD LIBS® • © 2009 Disney. Published by Price Stern Sloan,
a division of Penguin Young Readers Group, 345 Hudson Street, New York, NY 10014.

MAD LIBS® is fun to play with friends, but you can also play it by yourself! To begin with, DO NOT look at the story on the page below. Fill in the blanks on this page with the words called for. Then, using the words you have selected, fill in the blank spaces in the story.

Now you've created your own hilarious MAD LIBS® game!

PUFFLE PERSONALITIES, PART 1

ADJECTIVE _____

VERB _____

ADJECTIVE _____

ADJECTIVE _____

ADJECTIVE _____

ADJECTIVE _____

NOUN _____

ADJECTIVE _____

NOUN _____

ADJECTIVE _____

VERB _____

ADJECTIVE _____

ADJECTIVE _____

ADVERB _____

ADJECTIVE _____

VERB _____

MAD●LIBS®
PUFFLE PERSONALITIES, PART 1

Looking to adopt a puffle? These soft, _____ creatures
<u>ADJECTIVE</u>

make the perfect pets. Just _____ on over to the Pet
<u>VERB</u>

Shop, and you'll find many _____ puffles:
<u>ADJECTIVE</u>

Blue puffle: This _____ puffle is _____-
<u>ADJECTIVE</u>   <u>ADJECTIVE</u>

tempered, loyal, and _____. It loves to play with its
<u>ADJECTIVE</u>

_____ and is easy to take care of.
<u>NOUN</u>

Red puffle: Rockhopper discovered these adventurous,

_____ puffles on Rockhopper Island. They enjoy
<u>ADJECTIVE</u>

bowling and being shot out of a/an _____.
<u>NOUN</u>

Pink puffle: Always cheery and _____, these
<u>ADJECTIVE</u>

active puffles like to jump rope and _____ on the
<u>VERB</u>

trampoline. They especially love _____ exercise,
<u>ADJECTIVE</u>

including _____, long walks.
<u>ADJECTIVE</u>

Black puffle: Black puffles might seem _____
<u>ADVERB</u>

grumpy, but they're actually strong, _____ types who
<u>ADJECTIVE</u>

love to _____ on their skateboards.
<u>VERB</u>

FROM DISNEY CLUB PENGUIN™ MAD LIBS® • © 2009 Disney. Published by Price Stern Sloan,
a division of Penguin Young Readers Group, 345 Hudson Street, New York, NY 10014.

MAD LIBS® is fun to play with friends, but you can also play it by yourself! To begin with, DO NOT look at the story on the page below. Fill in the blanks on this page with the words called for. Then, using the words you have selected, fill in the blank spaces in the story.

Now you've created your own hilarious MAD LIBS® game!

PUFFLE PERSONALITIES, PART 2

PLURAL NOUN _____

ADJECTIVE _____

NOUN _____

ADJECTIVE _____

PLURAL NOUN _____

ADJECTIVE _____

NOUN _____

PLURAL NOUN _____

NOUN _____

ADJECTIVE _____

ADJECTIVE _____

ADJECTIVE _____

ADJECTIVE _____

MAD LIBS®
PUFFLE PERSONALITIES, PART 2

More puffles!

Green puffle: Green puffles are silly little _____. They

_____PLURAL NOUN_

are playful and _____, and they enjoy clowning around.

_____ADJECTIVE_

Their favorite activity is riding around on a/an _____.

_____NOUN_

Purple puffle: Purple puffles are known to act like

_____ divas. They are especially picky about

_____ADJECTIVE_

what kinds of _____ they eat. But they have a/an

_____PLURAL NOUN_

_____ sense of rhythm and they love to dance, dance,

____ADJECTIVE_

dance the _____ away under their disco ball.

_____NOUN_

Yellow puffle: These creative _____ are very artistic.

_____PLURAL NOUN_

Give them a canvas and _____ and these dreamers will

_____NOUN_

create a/an _____ painting.

_____ADJECTIVE_

White puffle: With one _____ breath this

_____ADJECTIVE_

_____ puffle can turn anything into ice. It loves to

_____ADJECTIVE_

ice-skate, and its personality is gentle yet _____.

_____ADJECTIVE_

FROM DISNEY CLUB PENGUIN™ MAD LIBS® • © 2009 Disney. Published by Price Stern Sloan,
a division of Penguin Young Readers Group, 345 Hudson Street, New York, NY 10014.

MAD LIBS® is fun to play with friends, but you can also play it by yourself! To begin with, DO NOT look at the story on the page below. Fill in the blanks on this page with the words called for. Then, using the words you have selected, fill in the blank spaces in the story.

Now you've created your own hilarious MAD LIBS® game!

GARY'S GADGETS

ADJECTIVE _____

PLURAL NOUN _____

ADJECTIVE _____

ADJECTIVE _____

PLURAL NOUN _____

NOUN _____

PLURAL NOUN _____

ADJECTIVE _____

PLURAL NOUN _____

NOUN _____

NOUN _____

ADJECTIVE _____

PLURAL NOUN _____

PLURAL NOUN _____

PLURAL NOUN _____

MAD LIBS®

GARY'S GADGETS

Gary the Gadget Guy, Club Penguin's _____ inventor,

ADJECTIVE

has created many useful _____. Here are a few of his

PLURAL NOUN

most _____ inventions:

ADJECTIVE

The Clock Tower: Located at the Snow Forts, this_____

ADJECTIVE

clock is powered by snow _____. Like all other clocks

PLURAL NOUN

in Club Penguin, it runs on Penguin Standard _____.

NOUN

This allows penguins from all over the world to pick times and places

to meet up with their fellow _____.

PLURAL NOUN

Pizzatron 3000: This _____ machine helps penguins

ADJECTIVE

make delicious, piping hot _____ in no time at all.

PLURAL NOUN

There is even an option to make _____ pizzas!

NOUN

AC 3000: This powerful _____ is a/an_____

NOUN   ADJECTIVE

air conditioner. It has been used to keep _____ from

PLURAL NOUN

melting and to create frozen _____. It came in especially

PLURAL NOUN

handy during Club Penguin's Festival of _____.

PLURAL NOUN

FROM DISNEY CLUB PENGUIN™ MAD LIBS® • © 2009 Disney. Published by Price Stern Sloan,
a division of Penguin Young Readers Group, 345 Hudson Street, New York, NY 10014.

MAD LIBS® is fun to play with friends, but you can also play it by yourself! To begin with, DO NOT look at the story on the page below. Fill in the blanks on this page with the words called for. Then, using the words you have selected, fill in the blank spaces in the story.

Now you've created your own hilarious MAD LIBS® game!

PARTY PENGUINS

NOUN _____

ADJECTIVE _____

ADJECTIVE _____

NOUN _____

ADJECTIVE _____

ADJECTIVE _____

VERB ENDING IN "ING" _____

NOUN _____

PLURAL NOUN _____

PART OF THE BODY (PLURAL) _____

NOUN _____

PLURAL NOUN _____

NOUN _____

ADJECTIVE _____

MAD LIBS®
PARTY PENGUINS

_____ Day is coming up and Club Penguin is
　　　NOUN

celebrating with a/an _____ island-wide party.
　　　　　　　　　　　　ADJECTIVE

You won't want to miss all the _____ action.
　　　　　　　　　　　　　　　　ADJECTIVE

The entire island will be decorated like a/an _____,
　　　　　　　　　　　　　　　　　　　　　　　　NOUN

and _____ music will be playing everywhere. There
　　　　ADJECTIVE

will be _____ activities happening around the island,
　　　　　ADJECTIVE

such as a/an _____ contest at the Dock and a/an
　　　　　　　VERB ENDING IN "ING"

_____ to play in at the Snow Forts. For the first time
　　　NOUN

ever, Club Penguin is giving away free _____ for
　　　　　　　　　　　　　　　　　　　　PLURAL NOUN

penguins to wear on their _____. If you desire,
　　　　　　　　　　　　　PART OF THE BODY (PLURAL)

you can even buy _____-themed clothes and
　　　　　　　　　　NOUN

accessories from the Penguin Style catalog. And in the Better Igloos

catalog, you'll even find furniture that looks like _____
　　　　　　　　　　　　　　　　　　　　　　　　　PLURAL NOUN

to put inside your igloo. It's Club Penguin's most exciting

_____ of the year. So come celebrate and have a really
　　　NOUN

_____ time!
　　　ADJECTIVE

MAD LIBS® is fun to play with friends, but you can also play it by yourself! To begin with, DO NOT look at the story on the page below. Fill in the blanks on this page with the words called for. Then, using the words you have selected, fill in the blank spaces in the story.

Now you've created your own hilarious MAD LIBS® game!

THE NEW PLAY, PART 1

NOUN _____

ADJECTIVE _____

ADJECTIVE _____

ADJECTIVE _____

ADJECTIVE _____

PART OF THE BODY _____

ADJECTIVE _____

NOUN _____

PLURAL NOUN _____

ADJECTIVE _____

NOUN _____

ADJECTIVE _____

NOUN _____

ADJECTIVE _____

NOUN _____

MAD LIBS®
THE NEW PLAY, PART 1

A sequel to the play *Quest for the Golden* _____ has
_{NOUN}

been written. Unfortunately, it is not _____ enough for
_{ADJECTIVE}

The Stage. But you and your _____ friends can read this
_{ADJECTIVE}

_____ play aloud, anyway.
_{ADJECTIVE}

Yukon: This _____ haunted castle sure seems dangerous
_{ADJECTIVE}

to me, Alaska. I don't think we should set _____ in such
_{PART OF THE BODY}

a/an _____ place.
_{ADJECTIVE}

Alaska: Stop being such a/an _____, Yukon. It's not
_{NOUN}

that scary. Besides, one of the most valuable _____ in
_{PLURAL NOUN}

the world is hidden here.

Yukon: You mean the _____ glow-in-the-dark puffle?
_{ADJECTIVE}

Alaska: Yes, and I bet it's right behind this secret _____ . . .
_{NOUN}

Ghost: *OOooOOoo!* Who enters my master's _____ lair?
_{ADJECTIVE}

Yukon: Eek! Alaska, let's get out of this _____!
_{NOUN}

Alaska: It's just a/an _____ ghost, Yukon. He couldn't
_{ADJECTIVE}

hurt a/an _____.
_{NOUN}

MAD LIBS® is fun to play with friends, but you can also play it by yourself! To begin with, DO NOT look at the story on the page below. Fill in the blanks on this page with the words called for. Then, using the words you have selected, fill in the blank spaces in the story.

Now you've created your own hilarious MAD LIBS® game!

THE NEW PLAY, PART 2

SILLY WORD _____

ADJECTIVE _____

EXCLAMATION _____

PLURAL NOUN _____

ADJECTIVE _____

ADJECTIVE _____

ADJECTIVE _____

NOUN _____

ADJECTIVE _____

ADJECTIVE _____

NOUN _____

ADJECTIVE _____

MAD LIBS®
THE NEW PLAY, PART 2

Ghost: You have awakened my master, Count _____.
SILLY WORD

Now you must face the _____ consequences.
ADJECTIVE

Yukon: _____! I am shaking in my _____!
EXCLAMATION   PLURAL NOUN

The Count: Who disturbs my _____ sleep?
ADJECTIVE

Alaska: We wanted to borrow your _____ puffle.
ADJECTIVE

The Count: First you vake me from my _____
ADJECTIVE

slumber, then you try and steal my prized _____?
NOUN

Get them, Ghostie! Don't let them escape vith my night-light!

Yukon: Your night-light? Alaska, this isn't a real glowing puffle. It's

just a night-light! Our _____ Count is afraid of the dark!
ADJECTIVE

The Count: Yes, I admit it. I vould never be able to sleep in this

haunted house vithout my _____ night-light.
ADJECTIVE

Alaska: Well, Yukon, our _____ is done here.
NOUN

On to more _____ adventures!
ADJECTIVE

Ghost: *OOooOOoo.* Thanks for stopping by!

FROM DISNEY CLUB PENGUIN™ MAD LIBS® • © 2009 Disney. Published by Price Stern Sloan,
a division of Penguin Young Readers Group, 345 Hudson Street, New York, NY 10014.

MAD LIBS® is fun to play with friends, but you can also play it by yourself! To begin with, DO NOT look at the story on the page below. Fill in the blanks on this page with the words called for. Then, using the words you have selected, fill in the blank spaces in the story.

Now you've created your own hilarious MAD LIBS® game!

PIZZA PARLOR SPECIALS

ADJECTIVE _____

PERSON IN ROOM _____

ADJECTIVE _____

ADJECTIVE _____

NOUN _____

NOUN _____

NOUN _____

PLURAL NOUN _____

ADJECTIVE _____

PLURAL NOUN _____

A PLACE _____

NOUN _____

ADJECTIVE _____

NOUN _____

TYPE OF LIQUID _____

VERB _____

ADJECTIVE _____

MAD LIBS®

PIZZA PARLOR SPECIALS

Greetings, _____ penguins! Welcome to the Pizza
                ADJECTIVE

Parlor. I'm _____, your _____ waiter. Let
            PERSON IN ROOM   ADJECTIVE

me tell you about today's _____ specials. We have a/an
                              ADJECTIVE

_____-lovers pizza topped with _____
      NOUN   NOUN

cheese, _____ fish, and _____. It's
              NOUN   PLURAL NOUN

delicious! We've also got a special _____ pizza with
                                         ADJECTIVE

extra cheese, plus _____ imported from (the)
                      PLURAL NOUN

_____, and a/an _____-stuffed crust. It's
    A PLACE   NOUN

a real treat. But first, can I get you something _____ to
                                                    ADJECTIVE

drink? We offer _____ soda and _____.
                    NOUN   TYPE OF LIQUID

I'll give you a moment to _____ about it. I'll be back to
                              VERB

take your _____ order.
              ADJECTIVE

FROM DISNEY CLUB PENGUIN™ MAD LIBS® • © 2009 Disney. Published by Price Stern Sloan,
a division of Penguin Young Readers Group, 345 Hudson Street, New York, NY 10014.

MAD LIBS® is fun to play with friends, but you can also play it by yourself! To begin with, DO NOT look at the story on the page below. Fill in the blanks on this page with the words called for. Then, using the words you have selected, fill in the blank spaces in the story.

Now you've created your own hilarious MAD LIBS® game!

WANTED!

ADJECTIVE _____

ADJECTIVE _____

NOUN _____

COLOR _____

ADJECTIVE _____

NOUN _____

NOUN _____

NOUN _____

ADJECTIVE _____

TYPE OF LIQUID _____

PLURAL NOUN _____

ADVERB _____

ADJECTIVE _____

MAD LIBS®
WANTED!

The following is a bulletin from the Penguin Secret Agency:

Please be on the lookout for the _____ suspects in an
ADJECTIVE

investigation, Herbert P. Bear, Esquire, and his _____
ADJECTIVE

accomplice, Klutzy. Herbert is described as a huge polar bear

with an angry _____ on his face. Klutzy is a/an
NOUN

_____ crab with _____ claws. Herbert
COLOR ADJECTIVE

came to Club Penguin when he left his native _____,
NOUN

Antarctica, and traveled by iceberg in search of a warmer

_____. Instead, he found Club Penguin—another
NOUN

freezing cold _____, full of _____
NOUN ADJECTIVE

penguins. As Herbert turned to paddle away, his iceberg

tipped and he was left stranded in the cold _____.
TYPE OF LIQUID

That's when Klutzy came along and rescued him. The two

have been _____ in mischief ever since.
PLURAL NOUN

Please _____ report any sighting of Herbert or
ADVERB

Klutzy. Both are clawed and potentially _____.
ADJECTIVE

MAD LIBS® is fun to play with friends, but you can also play it by yourself! To begin with, DO NOT look at the story on the page below. Fill in the blanks on this page with the words called for. Then, using the words you have selected, fill in the blank spaces in the story.

Now you've created your own hilarious MAD LIBS® game!

SENSEI'S WISDOM

ADJECTIVE _____

ADJECTIVE _____

ADJECTIVE _____

COLOR _____

NOUN _____

NOUN _____

NOUN _____

ADJECTIVE _____

VERB _____

ADJECTIVE _____

ADJECTIVE _____

ADJECTIVE _____

ADJECTIVE _____

ADJECTIVE _____

PART OF THE BODY (PLURAL) _____

SENSEI'S WISDOM

Sensei is a wise, _____ penguin. Here, a/an
ADJECTIVE

_____ ninja-in-training asks for some advice, and
ADJECTIVE

Sensei answers using the _____ art of haiku:
ADJECTIVE

Penguin: Sensei, I have earned a/an _____ belt playing
COLOR

_____-*Jitsu*. But trying to earn a black belt is putting
NOUN

my _____ to the test. What can I do to achieve my
NOUN

_____?
NOUN

Sensei: The road, it is _____.
ADJECTIVE

You must _____ and be patient.
VERB

Practice makes _____.
ADJECTIVE

Penguin: Will I ever be able to defeat you, oh _____
ADJECTIVE

one, and become a/an _____ ninja?
ADJECTIVE

Sensei: My _____ grasshopper.
ADJECTIVE

I am a/an _____ opponent.
ADJECTIVE

But it's in your _____.
PART OF THE BODY (PLURAL)

FROM DISNEY CLUB PENGUIN™ MAD LIBS® • © 2009 Disney. Published by Price Stern Sloan,
a division of Penguin Young Readers Group, 345 Hudson Street, New York, NY 10014.

MAD LIBS® is fun to play with friends, but you can also play it by yourself! To begin with, DO NOT look at the story on the page below. Fill in the blanks on this page with the words called for. Then, using the words you have selected, fill in the blank spaces in the story.

Now you've created your own hilarious MAD LIBS® game!

SECRET AGENT QUIZ

ADJECTIVE _____

ADJECTIVE _____

ADJECTIVE _____

ADJECTIVE _____

NOUN _____

PLURAL NOUN _____

NOUN _____

ADJECTIVE _____

ADVERB _____

ADVERB _____

PLURAL NOUN _____

A PLACE _____

NOUN _____

ADJECTIVE _____

NOUN _____

NOUN _____

MAD LIBS®

SECRET AGENT QUIZ

Have you got what it takes to join the _____ Penguin
ADJECTIVE

Secret Agency? Take this _____ quiz to find out.
ADJECTIVE

1. Pick a word to describe a secret agent: (a) _____,
ADJECTIVE

   (b) honest, or (c) _____
   ADJECTIVE

2. Pick the correct reason to report a penguin to the _____:
NOUN

   (a) throwing _____, (b) not accepting your
   PLURAL NOUN

   _____ request, (c) being _____
   NOUN   ADJECTIVE

3. What would you do if you saw some penguins breaking the rules?:

   (a) Yell _____ at them, (b) _____
   ADVERB   ADVERB

   report them, or (c) throw _____ at them.
   PLURAL NOUN

4. Why do you want to be a secret agent?: (a) I want to go to (the)

   _____, (b) I want a/an _____, or
   A PLACE   NOUN

   (c) I want to keep Club Penguin _____.
   ADJECTIVE

Thank you. Your application will be sent to the Club Penguin team for

review, and you will receive a spy _____ if you have
NOUN

been accepted into the _____ Secret Agency.
NOUN

MAD LIBS® is fun to play with friends, but you can also play it by yourself! To begin with, DO NOT look at the story on the page below. Fill in the blanks on this page with the words called for. Then, using the words you have selected, fill in the blank spaces in the story.

Now you've created your own hilarious MAD LIBS® game!

INCREDIBLE IGLOO

ADJECTIVE _____

PLURAL NOUN _____

ADJECTIVE _____

NOUN _____

ADJECTIVE _____

NOUN _____

NOUN _____

NOUN _____

ADJECTIVE _____

PART OF THE BODY (PLURAL) _____

NOUN _____

ADJECTIVE _____

NOUN _____

NUMBER_____

ADJECTIVE _____

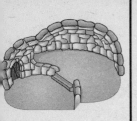

MAD LIBS®
INCREDIBLE IGLOO

Want your igloo to reveal your _____ personality?
                                        ADJECTIVE

Why not upgrade it? Instead of a regular igloo made of

_____, you can live in a/an _____ castle
    PLURAL NOUN   ADJECTIVE

or a snow _____. Once you've upgraded, add some
                NOUN

_____ furniture, like an inflatable _____
    ADJECTIVE   NOUN

or a poster of your favorite _____. Another way to
                                    NOUN

update your _____ is to put in some cool flooring,
                NOUN

like _____ tile or plush carpets that feel soft under
        ADJECTIVE

flippered _____. Another great way to make your
            PART OF THE BODY (PLURAL)

_____ homier is to add furry, _____ pets.
    NOUN   ADJECTIVE

That's right—puffles! There's nothing like cuddling up to a furry

_____ when you want to feel right at home. When
    NOUN

all is said and done, there are a million and _____
                                                    NUMBER

ways to personalize your igloo. After all, there's no place like

home, _____ home!
        ADJECTIVE

FROM DISNEY CLUB PENGUIN™ MAD LIBS® • © 2009 Disney. Published by Price Stern Sloan,
a division of Penguin Young Readers Group, 345 Hudson Street, New York, NY 10014.

MAD LIBS® is fun to play with friends, but you can also play it by yourself! To begin with, DO NOT look at the story on the page below. Fill in the blanks on this page with the words called for. Then, using the words you have selected, fill in the blank spaces in the story.

Now you've created your own hilarious MAD LIBS® game!

RESCUE SQUAD, TO THE RESCUE!

ADJECTIVE _____

ADJECTIVE _____

ADJECTIVE _____

PART OF THE BODY (PLURAL) _____

ADJECTIVE _____

ADVERB _____

NOUN _____

PLURAL NOUN _____

NOUN _____

A PLACE _____

ADJECTIVE _____

PLURAL NOUN _____

ADVERB _____

ADJECTIVE _____

NOUN _____

NOUN _____

ADJECTIVE _____

ADJECTIVE _____

MAD☺LIBS®
RESCUE SQUAD, TO THE RESCUE!

It was a bright, _____ day on Club Penguin. I was just
ADJECTIVE

starting my Rescue Squad duties at the _____ Ski Hill
ADJECTIVE

when suddenly, I felt a/an _____ rumbling beneath
ADJECTIVE

my _____. I knew immediately that a/an
PART OF THE BODY (PLURAL)

_____ avalanche was coming! I shifted _____
ADJECTIVE   ADVERB

into rescue mode. As a Rescue Squad _____, I had
NOUN

to save all the sledding _____ before the snow crashed
PLURAL NOUN

down the _____ Hill. "Everyone, follow me to (the)
NOUN

_____!" I shouted. All the _____
A PLACE   ADJECTIVE

penguins raced after me as we ran from the tumbling, rumbling

_____. As we headed _____ to safety,
PLURAL NOUN   ADVERB

I took one scared, _____ penguin after another
ADJECTIVE

to the Iceberg—far out of harm's _____. Not a single
NOUN

_____ was hurt. That _____ avalanche
NOUN   ADJECTIVE

was no match for an experienced, _____ member of
ADJECTIVE

the Rescue Squad!

MAD LIBS® is fun to play with friends, but you can also play it by yourself! To begin with, DO NOT look at the story on the page below. Fill in the blanks on this page with the words called for. Then, using the words you have selected, fill in the blank spaces in the story.

Now you've created your own hilarious MAD LIBS® game!

ROCKING WITH THE PENGUIN BAND

VERB ENDING IN "ING" _____

ADJECTIVE _____

PART OF THE BODY (PLURAL) _____

PLURAL NOUN _____

ADJECTIVE _____

PART OF THE BODY _____

NOUN _____

NOUN _____

PART OF THE BODY _____

ADVERB _____

NUMBER _____

VERB (PAST TENSE) _____

ADJECTIVE _____

The crowd of penguins at the Lighthouse was _____

VERB ENDING IN "ING"

with anticipation, waiting for their favorite band to come

onstage. Finally, a/an _____ penguin walked

ADJECTIVE

onstage and said, "Please put your _____

PART OF THE BODY (PLURAL)

together for the Penguin Band!" Applause erupted as four

_____ wearing cowboy hats took to the stage.

PLURAL NOUN

Franky, wearing _____ sneakers, slung his guitar

ADJECTIVE

over his _____. Stompin' Bob, looking cool as

PART OF THE BODY

a/an _____ in a pair of sunglasses, strapped on his

NOUN

bass _____. Petey K, with his accordion around

NOUN

his _____, pushed his glasses up on his beak and

PART OF THE BODY

smiled _____ at the audience. Then G Billy sat

ADVERB

behind the drums and counted down: "Five, four, three, two,

_____!" The band started rocking away, and the

NUMBER

audience _____. It was the beginning of another

VERB (PAST TENSE)

_____ performance by the Penguin Band!

ADJECTIVE

FROM DISNEY CLUB PENGUIN™ MAD LIBS® • © 2009 Disney. Published by Price Stern Sloan,
a division of Penguin Young Readers Group, 345 Hudson Street, New York, NY 10014.

MAD LIBS® is fun to play with friends, but you can also play it by yourself! To begin with, DO NOT look at the story on the page below. Fill in the blanks on this page with the words called for. Then, using the words you have selected, fill in the blank spaces in the story.

Now you've created your own hilarious MAD LIBS® game!

COFFEE TALK

NOUN _____

NOUN _____

ADJECTIVE _____

ADJECTIVE _____

TYPE OF LIQUID _____

ADJECTIVE _____

NOUN _____

ADJECTIVE _____

PART OF THE BODY (PLURAL) _____

COLOR _____

ADVERB _____

ADJECTIVE _____

NOUN _____

NOUN _____

ADJECTIVE _____

MAD LIBS®

COFFEE TALK

I was sitting on a/an _____ at the Coffee Shop, reading
                              NOUN

The Club _____ *Times*, when a/an _____
                  NOUN   ADJECTIVE

penguin plopped down next to me. "Hi!" she said in a/an

_____ voice, taking a sip of her steaming cup of
      ADJECTIVE

_____. "What are you reading about?" I smiled back.
  TYPE OF LIQUID

"I'm reading about *Card-Jitsu*," I said. "This article has some

_____ tips. I'm not very good at it, but I love to
      ADJECTIVE

play!" "I love _____-*Jitsu*, too!" she said. "I just became
                      NOUN

a/an _____ ninja." My _____
          ADJECTIVE   PART OF THE BODY (PLURAL)

turned pink with embarrassment as I admitted, "I'm only a/an

_____ belt. But maybe you could help me!" She
      COLOR

nodded _____. "Sure! Why don't we go over to the Dojo?
          ADVERB

I've got some _____ tricks up my _____
                    ADJECTIVE   NOUN

that I can show you." So my new _____ and I waddled
                                          NOUN

over to the Dojo. It was just another _____ day of
                                              ADJECTIVE

making new friends on Club Penguin!

FROM DISNEY CLUB PENGUIN™ MAD LIBS® • © 2009 Disney. Published by Price Stern Sloan,
a division of Penguin Young Readers Group, 345 Hudson Street, New York, NY 10014.

MAD LIBS® is fun to play with friends, but you can also play it by yourself! To begin with, DO NOT look at the story on the page below. Fill in the blanks on this page with the words called for. Then, using the words you have selected, fill in the blank spaces in the story.

Now you've created your own hilarious MAD LIBS® game!

THE BIG GAME

ADJECTIVE _____

PLURAL NOUN _____

PART OF THE BODY _____

NOUN _____

ADJECTIVE _____

NOUN _____

NUMBER _____

NOUN _____

ADVERB _____

NOUN _____

NOUN _____

VERB ENDING IN "S" _____

NOUN _____

NOUN _____

MAD LIBS®
THE BIG GAME

The Red Team and the Blue Team are playing a/an _____

ADJECTIVE

hockey game at the Ice Rink. The following is the announcers'

play-by-play, to be read aloud by two _____:

PLURAL NOUN

Announcer #1: It's neck and _____ between the Red

PART OF THE BODY

Team and the Blue Team. It's any _____'s guess who

NOUN

will win this _____ game.

ADJECTIVE

Announcer #2: Yes, it's a tied _____, with just

NOUN

_____ seconds left to play.

NUMBER

Announcer #1: The star _____ for the Red Team

NOUN

has got the puck, and she's skating _____ toward

ADVERB

the Blue Team's _____. She passes the puck to the

NOUN

_____.

NOUN

Announcer #2: He shoots, he _____! The

VERB ENDING IN "S"

_____ is going wild! The Red Team has won the

NOUN

_____!

NOUN

FROM DISNEY CLUB PENGUIN™ MAD LIBS® • © 2009 Disney. Published by Price Stern Sloan,
a division of Penguin Young Readers Group, 345 Hudson Street, New York, NY 10014.

MAD LIBS® is fun to play with friends, but you can also play it by yourself! To begin with, DO NOT look at the story on the page below. Fill in the blanks on this page with the words called for. Then, using the words you have selected, fill in the blank spaces in the story.

Now you've created your own hilarious MAD LIBS® game!

PARTY AT MY IGLOO!

PLURAL NOUN _____

ARTICLE OF CLOTHING (PLURAL) _____

ADJECTIVE _____

NOUN _____

ADJECTIVE _____

ADJECTIVE _____

PLURAL NOUN _____

NOUN _____

NOUN _____

VERB _____

ADJECTIVE _____

PLURAL NOUN _____

NOUN _____

MAD LIBS®
PARTY AT MY IGLOO!

All right, party _____—put on your party
　　　　　　　　　　PLURAL NOUN

_____. There's a/an _____
ARTICLE OF CLOTHING (PLURAL)　　　　　　　　　ADJECTIVE

party at my igloo! Every _____ on Club Penguin
　　　　　　　　　　　　　　　NOUN

is invited—and their _____ puffles, too. I've decorated
　　　　　　　　　　ADJECTIVE

my igloo with _____ streamers and I've blown
　　　　　　　ADJECTIVE

up lots of colorful _____. There will be snacks like
　　　　　　　　　PLURAL NOUN

squid and _____ pizza from the Pizza Parlor and
　　　　　　NOUN

_____ soda to drink. We'll play games like hide-
　　NOUN

and-_____, and we'll have a contest to see who the
　　　VERB

most _____ dancer is. Yep, we're going to party until
　　ADJECTIVE

the _____ come home. You'll have the time of your
　　PLURAL NOUN

_____!
　NOUN

FROM DISNEY CLUB PENGUIN™ MAD LIBS® • © 2009 Disney. Published by Price Stern Sloan,
a division of Penguin Young Readers Group, 345 Hudson Street, New York, NY 10014.

MAD LIBS® is fun to play with friends, but you can also play it by yourself! To begin with, DO NOT look at the story on the page below. Fill in the blanks on this page with the words called for. Then, using the words you have selected, fill in the blank spaces in the story.

Now you've created your own hilarious MAD LIBS® game!

DANCE WITH CADENCE

NOUN _____

ADJECTIVE _____

PLURAL NOUN _____

VERB _____

NOUN _____

PLURAL NOUN _____

NOUN _____

PART OF THE BODY (PLURAL) _____

PART OF THE BODY (PLURAL) _____

ADJECTIVE _____

ADJECTIVE _____

ADJECTIVE _____

NOUN _____

PART OF THE BODY _____

NOUN _____

VERB _____

NOUN _____

ADJECTIVE _____

NOUN _____

MAD LIBS®

DANCE WITH CADENCE

Yo, Cadence here! Welcome to the _____ Club. Are
NOUN

you ready for a/an _____ dance lesson? Great. I'll teach
ADJECTIVE

you some basic _____. Want to _____
PLURAL NOUN   VERB

to the hit song "Epic _____"? It's one of my favorites!
NOUN

Okay, first _____ first. This move is called "the
PLURAL NOUN

_____." Try wiggling your _____
NOUN   PART OF THE BODY (PLURAL)

and waving your _____ in the air. Hey, that looks
PART OF THE BODY (PLURAL)

_____! You're a/an _____ learner.
ADJECTIVE   ADJECTIVE

Next, let's try "the _____ _____."
ADJECTIVE   NOUN

It's a popular move here at the Night Club. You just bob

your _____ to the music and twirl like a/an
PART OF THE BODY

_____. You got it! Way to go! I think you're ready
NOUN

to _____ with the best of them. It's time to get out
VERB

on the dance floor and face the _____. Just bust out
NOUN

your most _____ moves, and show them what you can
ADJECTIVE

do. You're a natural _____!
NOUN

FROM DISNEY CLUB PENGUIN™ MAD LIBS® • © 2009 Disney. Published by Price Stern Sloan,
a division of Penguin Young Readers Group, 345 Hudson Street, New York, NY 10014.

MAD LIBS® is fun to play with friends, but you can also play it by yourself! To begin with, DO NOT look at the story on the page below. Fill in the blanks on this page with the words called for. Then, using the words you have selected, fill in the blank spaces in the story.

Now you've created your own hilarious MAD LIBS® game!

SNOWBALL FIGHT!

ADJECTIVE _____

ADJECTIVE _____

PLURAL NOUN _____

NOUN _____

ADJECTIVE _____

NOUN _____

PLURAL NOUN _____

NOUN _____

PLURAL NOUN _____

ADJECTIVE _____

NOUN _____

ADJECTIVE _____

ADJECTIVE _____

VERB _____

PLURAL NOUN _____

MAD LIBS®

SNOWBALL FIGHT!

So you want to have a/an _____ snowball fight? Here
_____ ADJECTIVE

are some _____ instructions to get you started:
_____ ADJECTIVE

1. Go around Club Penguin, telling your friends and

_____ to come to the _____ Forts. Say
PLURAL NOUN   NOUN

something like, "_____ snow-_____
_____ ADJECTIVE   NOUN

fight at the Snow _____! It's going to be the best
PLURAL NOUN

_____ ever!"
NOUN

2. Once everyone arrives, gather the _____ into two
PLURAL NOUN

_____ teams. You could have a Red and a
ADJECTIVE

Blue Team, or each team could wear matching outfits, like

_____ hats and _____ shirts.
NOUN   ADJECTIVE

3. When all the _____ penguins are in their places,
ADJECTIVE

say, "On your mark, get set, _____!"
VERB

4. Throw snow-_____!
PLURAL NOUN

This book is published by

PSS!

PRICE STERN SLOAN

whose other splendid titles include
such literary classics as